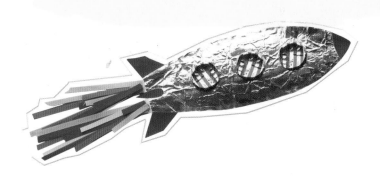

BLAST OFF!
JUPITER

Helen and David Orme

Copyright © ticktock Entertainment Ltd 2007
First published in Great Britain in 2006 by ticktock Media Ltd.,
Unit 2, Orchard Business Centre, North Farm Road,
Tunbridge Wells, Kent, TN2 3XF

ticktock project editor: Julia Adams
ticktock project designer: Emma Randall

We would like to thank: Sandra Voss, Tim Bones, James Powell,
Indexing Specialists (UK) Ltd.

ISBN 978 1 84696 052 9

A CIP catalogue record for this book is available from the British Library.

Picture credits
t=top, b=bottom, c=centre, l-left, r=right, bg=background
Corbis: 15tr; NASA: 1tl, 1br, 7tr, 7bl, 8br, 9tr, 9c, 9br, 10bl, 11tl, 12br, 13tc, 13cl (inset), 13cr, 17br, 17bc, 18tl, 18cl, 18cr, 18br,
19tl, 19cl (inset), 19cl, 19cr, 19bl, 20c, 22; Scientce Photo Library: front cover, 4/5bg (original), 12cr, 13tr, 13cl, 13br;
Shutterstock: 2/3bg, 7c, 16bc, 23tr, 24bg; ticktock picture archive: 5tr, 6/7bg, 6bl, 10/11bg, 10c, 14/15bg, 14c, 15bl, 16t,
16br, 17tl, 17tc, 18/19bg, 21tr, 21bl, 22/23bg, 23cl, 23brr

Every effort has been made to trace the copyright holders, and we apologise in advance for any unintentional omissions.
We would be pleased to insert the appropriate acknowledgements in any subsequent edition of this publication.

Contents

There are eight planets in our **solar system**. The planets travel around the Sun. Jupiter is the fifth planet from the Sun.

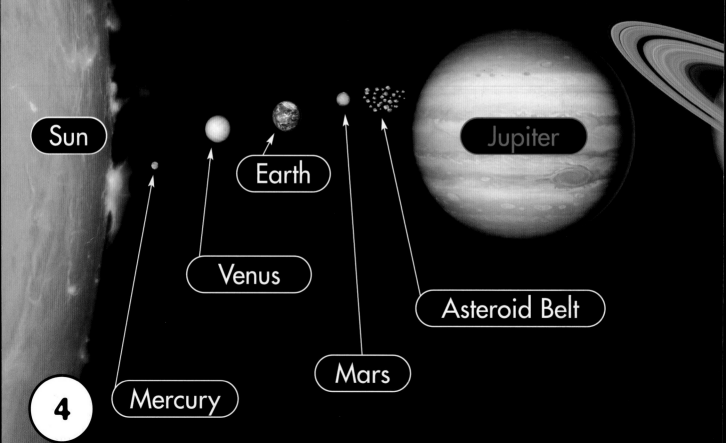

Sun

Earth

Venus

Jupiter

Asteroid Belt

Mars

Mercury

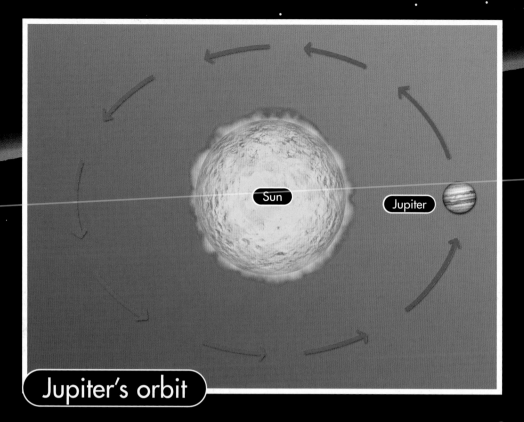

Jupiter's orbit

Jupiter travels around the Sun once every 12 **Earth years**. This journey is called its **orbit**. The time it takes for a planet to travel around the Sun once is called a **year**.

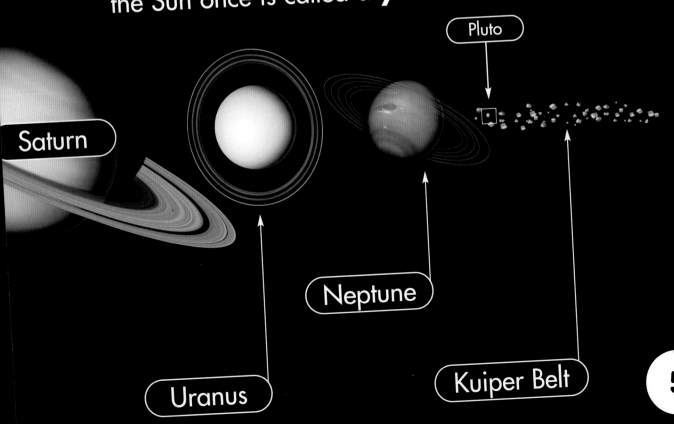

Pluto

Saturn

Neptune

Uranus

Kuiper Belt

Planet Facts

Jupiter is the biggest known planet in the **solar system**. It has a rocky centre, but the rest of the planet is made of **hydrogen gas**.

rocky centre

liquid

gas

inside Jupiter

Deep inside Jupiter, the hydrogen changes. It is a light gas at the surface. Deeper inside, it becomes **liquid**. The centre of Jupiter is made of solid hydrogen, rock and metal.

Jupiter is made of the same material as the Sun.

Jupiter

Jupiter is the biggest planet in the solar system. More than 1300 Earths could fit inside Jupiter.

142,984 kilometres

12,756 km

Earth

Planets are always spinning. A **day** is the time it takes a planet to spin around once. A day on Jupiter is the same length as 10 hours on Earth.

Jupiter is the fastest spinning planet in the solar system!

Jupiter spins at 13 kilometres per second! Spinning at such a high speed makes Jupiter a very stormy planet.

Winds blow in different directions on Jupiter. Some winds blow towards the planet to form the dark bands. Other winds blow away from Jupiter to form the light bands.

The winds on Jupiter can move at over 595 km per hour! This photo gives a close-up look at the mix of different winds on Jupiter.

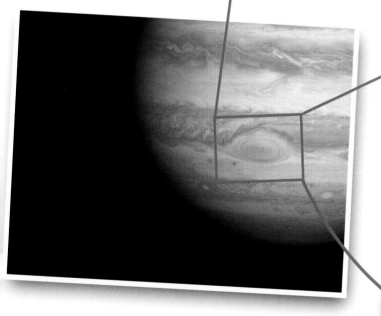

Storms on Jupiter can last for a long time. One huge storm has been raging for at least three hundred years!

We can see this storm in these photographs. It is called 'the great red spot'.

Moons and Rings

Jupiter has over 60 known moons! Our Earth only has one. Jupiter also has rings made of dust. The moons and the dust **orbit** Jupiter.

Jupiter's moons and rings of dust all orbit the planet in the same direction.

Jupiter

Moons

Rings

Meteorite

The dust was probably knocked off Jupiter's moons when they were hit by **meteorites**.

Io
3,642 km

Europa
3,121 km

Callisto

Ganymede
4,820 km

5,261 km

3,476 km

Most of Jupiter's moons are very small.

Jupiter's four largest moons are called Galilean moons, because they were discovered in 1610 by the **astronomer** Galileo Galilei.

This picture shows how big Jupiter's moons are compared to the Earth's moon and Jupiter itself.

Jupiter's Amazing Moons

Scientists have used **space probes** to study Jupiter's four largest moons. The drawings on these pages show what the surfaces of the moons look like.

Io is covered with **volcanoes**. It has more volcanoes than any other planet or moon in the **solar system.** The surface of Io is always changing.

Jupiter

Volcano

Io

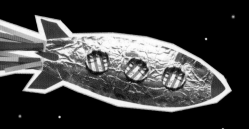

Europa is covered with a thick layer of ice. Some scientists think that there is an ocean of **liquid** water under the ice.

Jupiter

Europa

ice

Jupiter

rocky surface

Ganymede

Ganymede is the largest moon in the solar system. Ganymede's centre is made of rock. It is covered with a mixture of rock and ice.

Callisto is covered with **craters**. **Astronomers** think that nothing has changed on the surface of Callisto for 4 billion years!

Callisto

Crater

Jupiter in History

People have always known about Jupiter because it is such a bright object in the sky.

This drawing shows the ancient Greek **astronomer** Ptolemy. He lived over 1,800 years ago. Ptolemy studied Jupiter without using a telescope.

This is a statue of Jupiter. The ancient Romans believed Jupiter was the chief of their gods. They named the planet after Jupiter because it is the biggest planet in the **solar system**.

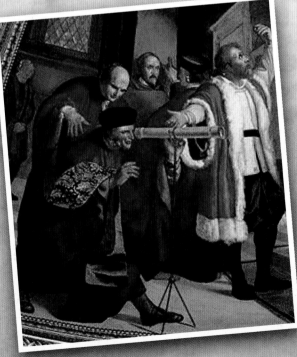

This is a painting of the Italian astronomer Galileo Galilei. He built one of the first telescopes in 1609. He used the telescope to discover Jupiter's four largest moons.

What Can We See?

Jupiter is one of the brightest objects in the sky. We can see Jupiter without a telescope or binoculars.

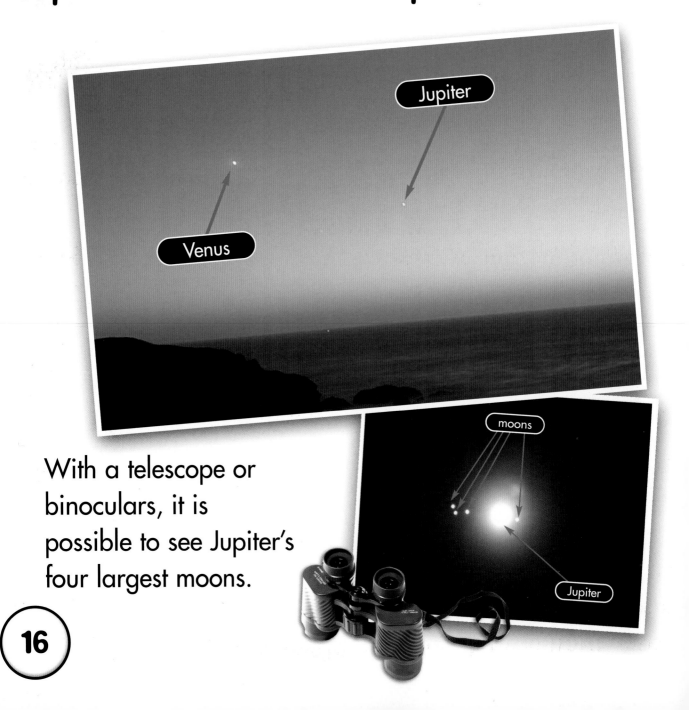

Jupiter

Venus

moons

Jupiter

With a telescope or binoculars, it is possible to see Jupiter's four largest moons.

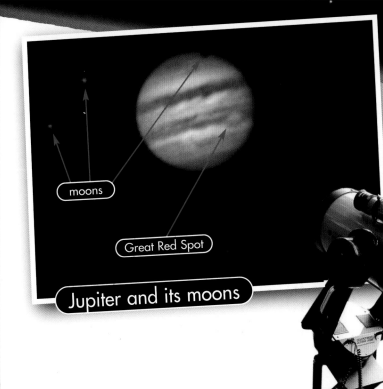

moons

Great Red Spot

Jupiter and its moons

With a larger telescope, we can see more of Jupiter's surface. We may even be able to see the Great Red Spot.

This photo of Jupiter was taken by the Hubble Space Telescope. The Hubble Telescope is out in space. It is in **orbit** around the Earth. It sends us photos that are really clear, like this one.

Missions to Jupiter

No person has ever travelled to Jupiter, but many **space probes** have been to the planet.

Pioneer 10

The first space mission to Jupiter was Pioneer 10. It flew past Jupiter in 1973. It took the first close-up photographs of the planet.

Jupiter's atmosphere

Jupiter

Voyagers 1 and 2 passed by Jupiter in 1979. They took photographs of the planet's **atmosphere**, its rings and its moons.

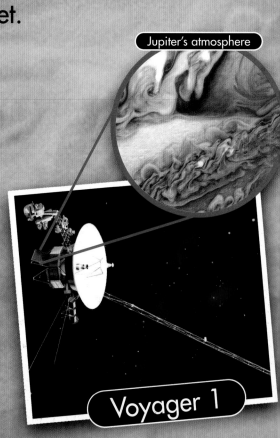

Voyager 1

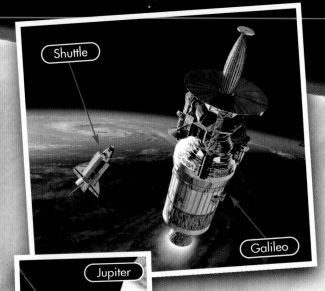

Shuttle

Galileo

Jupiter

Galileo in orbit

In 1989, the space probe Galileo was carried into space by a **space shuttle**. After the shuttle left Earth's atmosphere, it launched Galileo off into space towards Jupiter. Galileo flew through space and then went into **orbit** around Jupiter.

Galileo took pictures of the **volcanoes** on Io...

volcano

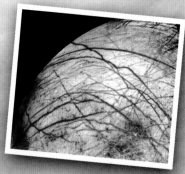

...and the icy surface of Europa.

Galileo also took this photo of the Great Red Spot.

Looking for Life

Because life as we know it is only possible on a planet that has **liquid** water, **astronomers** always look for water on planets.

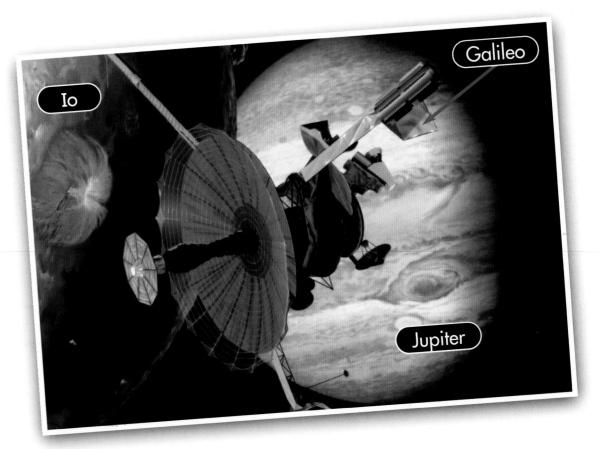

Io

Galileo

Jupiter

Jupiter has a very thick **atmosphere** and no solid surface. Scientists didn't expect to find water or life on the planet. But the Galileo **space probe** sent back exciting information about Jupiter's moon Europa.

Galileo's photographs of Europa show that the surface is covered in cracked ice.

Scientists think there might be an ocean of liquid water underneath the ice.

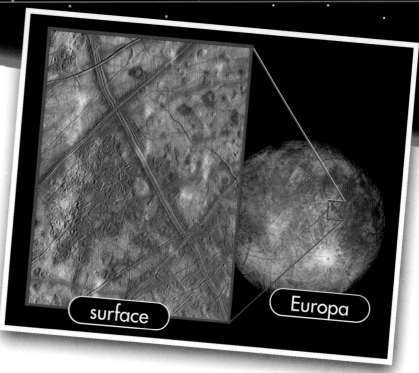

surface

Europa

They think the water may be heated by underwater **volcanoes**. This photograph shows an underwater volcano on Earth.

Scientists think that Europa might be a really good place to look for life.

hot gas

Future Missions

Scientists would like to send a **space probe** to land on Europa to look for life. This mission would be very difficult.

The probe would have to drill down through the ice on Europa to see what was underneath, as shown in this drawing.

Earth has a place where scientists can practise the mission to Europa. That place is in Antarctica, near the South Pole.

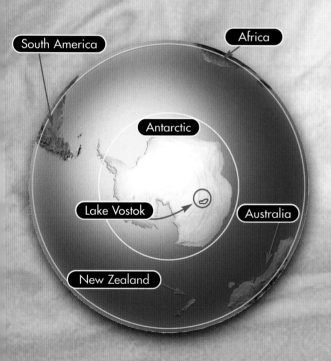

South America

Africa

Antarctic

Lake Vostok

Australia

New Zealand

Lake Vostok is a lake in the Antarctic that has been trapped under the ice for millions of years. The ice here is over 3 km thick!

Scientists are drilling through the ice at Lake Vostok to see what is in the water. Maybe one day they will try to do the same thing on Europa!

the scientists' camp

23

Glossary

Asteroid A rocky object that orbits the Sun. Most asteroids orbit the Sun between Mars and Jupiter.

Astronomer A person who studies space, often using telescopes.

Atmosphere The gases that surround a star, planet or moon.

Craters Holes in the surface of a planet or a moon. They are made either by a volcano or when a rock from space crashes into the surface and leaves a deep dent.

Day A day is the time it takes a planet to spin around once. A day on Earth is 24 hours long.

Earth years A year is the time it takes for a planet to orbit the Sun. An Earth year is 365 days long.

Hydrogen gas A very light gas. The Sun is also made of Hydrogen.

Liquid Something that flows easily.

Meteorites Pieces of rock that travel through space at high speed and crash into planets.

Orbit The path that a planet or other object takes around the Sun, or a satellite takes around a planet.

Solar system The Sun and everything that is in orbit around it.

Space probe A spacecraft sent from Earth to explore the solar system. It can collect samples and take pictures.

Space shuttle An aircraft that can carry astronauts and machines into space.

Volcanoes Mountains where the hot, liquid inside of a planet bursts to the surface.

Year The time it takes a planet to orbit the Sun.
A year on Jupiter lasts as long as 12 Earth years!

Index